A Guide to Kos 2024

Exploring the Traditions, Flavors, and Beauty of an Aegean Island

Nielsen Frye

Table of Contents

Lambi Beach
Recently viewed
Nerantzia Castle
Κάστρο Νεραντζιάς
Temporarily closed
Kos
Κως
C Food & Mood
Kalimnos - Kos
Kos - Rodos
Bodrum
PLATANI
ΠΛΑΤΑΝΙ
KAKO PINARI
ΚΑΚΟ ΠΡΙΝΑΡΙ
PARADISI
ΠΑΡΑΔΕΙΣΙ
GIAPILI
ΓΙΑΠΙΛΗ
Καταφύγιο
Φυσιολατρικου...
Paralia
Thermes
Προφήτης
αχαρίας ο Μικρός
Hidden beach

Chapter 1: Introduction to Kos

Overview of Kos

Nestled in the southeastern Aegean Sea, Kos is one of the Dodecanese islands, known for its blend of rich history, stunning landscapes, and welcoming atmosphere. The island spans just over 40 kilometers in length and 8 kilometers in width, making it easy for visitors to explore its charming villages, archaeological wonders, and pristine beaches. Kos is characterized by rolling hills, fertile plains, and a coastline that shifts from golden sand to rugged, dramatic cliffs, offering something for every kind of traveler.

Kos holds a significant place in history. The island is famously the birthplace of Hippocrates, the father of modern medicine, whose influence can still be felt today. The ancient Asklepion, one of the most important healing temples of antiquity, draws visitors from across the globe. Kos has been shaped by a variety of cultures over centuries, from the Romans and Byzantines to the Venetians and Ottomans, all leaving their mark in the form of ancient ruins, castles, and charming architecture.

Why visit in 2024?

Kos is a dynamic island that is constantly evolving, and 2024 promises to be an exciting year to visit. Several new attractions and experiences are set to open, catering to both first-time visitors and seasoned travelers. A fresh wave of boutique hotels and eco-friendly accommodations will debut, offering stylish yet sustainable lodging. For history enthusiasts, ongoing archaeological projects are expected to uncover new finds that will add further depth to the island's already impressive historical landscape.

In 2024, Kos will also host a variety of festivals and cultural events, celebrating both ancient traditions and modern Greek life. Highlights include the Kos Hippocrates Festival, paying homage to the island's most famous son, and the Zia Village Summer Festival, featuring local music, food, and crafts. The island's vineyards and wineries will be more accessible than ever, with special tours and tastings that allow visitors to sample Kos's blossoming wine scene.

What truly sets Kos apart is its ability to combine the best of Greece: the charm of a small island with the conveniences of a larger destination. From its secluded beaches and traditional villages to its vibrant nightlife and array of outdoor activities, Kos strikes the perfect balance between relaxation and adventure. Whether you're a history buff, a foodie, or simply looking to bask in the island's natural beauty, Kos in 2024 offers something for everyone.

Chapter 2: Practical Information

Getting to Kos (flights, ferries, and transport)

Kos is well-connected to both mainland Greece and other parts of Europe, making it relatively easy for travelers to reach the island. Whether arriving by plane or ferry, visitors have a range of options depending on their location and preferences.

Flights to Kos

The main airport on the island is Kos International Airport (KGS), also known as "Hippocrates Airport." Located just 24 kilometers from Kos Town, it serves as the primary gateway for international and domestic flights.

Nearest major cities and flight duration:

Athens: A direct flight from Athens International Airport (ATH) takes about 1 hour.

London: Flights from London airports (Heathrow, Gatwick, or Stansted) take approximately 4 hours.

Berlin: Direct flights from Berlin to Kos take around 3 hours.

Rome: Flights from Rome to Kos typically last about 2.5 hours.

Vienna: A direct flight from Vienna takes approximately 2 hours.

Several European airlines, including Aegean Airlines, Ryanair, EasyJet, and TUI, offer regular seasonal flights to Kos from cities across Europe. During the summer months, flights are more frequent, especially from popular tourist hubs like Germany, the UK, and Italy.

Ferries to Kos

If you prefer to arrive by sea, ferries to Kos are available from several locations in mainland Greece and neighboring islands.

From mainland Greece:

Piraeus (Athens): Ferries depart daily from Piraeus, taking about 10 to 12 hours to reach Kos. Operators like Blue Star Ferries offer comfortable journeys with a range of amenities on board, including cabins for overnight travel.

From nearby islands:

Rhodes: Frequent ferry connections between Rhodes and Kos, with travel times around 2 to 3 hours. Several operators, including Dodekanisos Seaways, provide these routes.

Kalymnos: A short 30-minute ferry ride connects Kos with Kalymnos, making it an ideal day-trip destination.

Patmos, Leros, and Nisyros: Other Dodecanese islands like Patmos and Leros are connected by ferries to Kos, with travel times varying between 1 and 4 hours, depending on the route and operator.

Ferry schedules are more frequent in the summer months and can be booked in advance through operators such as Blue Star Ferries and Dodekanisos Seaways.

Transport from the Airport or Port

Once you arrive in Kos, getting from the airport or ferry port to your accommodation is straightforward, with several transport options available.

Taxis: Taxis are readily available at Kos International Airport and the ferry port in Kos Town. The ride from the airport to Kos Town typically costs around €35 to €45, depending on your final destination. You can hail a taxi outside the arrivals area or pre-book one for convenience.

Buses: The island's bus system is operated by KTEL Kos and provides reliable, low-cost services from the airport to Kos Town and other major destinations. A bus from the airport to Kos Town takes around 30 minutes and costs approximately €3 to €5. There are also bus routes connecting the ferry port to popular towns and beaches.

Car Rentals: Renting a car is a popular option for travelers who want the flexibility to explore the island at their own pace. Several international and local car rental companies, including Avis, Hertz, and Kosmos Rent a Car, operate at the airport and ferry port. Pre-booking a rental car is recommended, especially during peak tourist season.

Shuttle Services: Some hotels offer shuttle services from the airport or port directly to your accommodation. Check with your hotel in advance to see if this option is available.

Visa requirements

Greece, including the island of Kos, is part of the Schengen Area, which means travelers from many countries can visit without a visa for short stays. However, the exact visa requirements depend on your nationality and the purpose of your visit.

Visa-Free Travel

EU/EEA Citizens: Citizens of European Union (EU) and European Economic Area (EEA) countries do not need a visa to visit Kos or any part of Greece. They can travel freely and stay for as long as they like, as Greece is part of the EU.

Schengen Area Visitors: Citizens from countries that are part of the Schengen Agreement can enter Greece without a visa for stays of up to 90 days within a 180-day period. This applies to countries like Switzerland, Norway, and Iceland, among others.

Visa Waiver Countries: Nationals from visa-exempt countries, such as the United States, Canada, Australia, Japan, the UK, and many others, can also visit Kos and Greece for up to 90 days within a 180-day period without requiring a visa. However, starting in 2024, travelers from visa-exempt countries will need to apply for an ETIAS (European Travel Information and Authorization System), a new pre-authorization system for entering Schengen countries. The ETIAS is expected to be a simple, online process that takes only minutes to complete.

Visa Required

Non-Schengen and Non-Visa Exempt Countries: Visitors from countries that are not part of the Schengen Area and do not have visa-waiver agreements with Greece will need to apply for a Schengen visa. This includes many African, Middle Eastern, and Asian countries.

How to Obtain a Schengen Visa:

Documents Needed:

1. A completed Schengen visa application form.
2. A valid passport with at least two blank pages and valid for at least three months beyond the intended stay.
3. Two passport-sized photos.
4. Proof of travel (round-trip flight booking or travel itinerary).
5. Travel insurance covering up to €30,000 for medical emergencies.
6. Proof of accommodation (hotel reservations or an invitation letter if staying with friends/family).

7. Proof of sufficient funds (bank statements or proof of sponsorship).

Application Process:

Schengen visa applications are submitted to the Greek embassy or consulate in your country of residence.

Processing time typically takes 15 calendar days, but it's advised to apply well in advance of your trip.

Fees for a Schengen visa are usually around €80 for adults, but may vary depending on the applicant's nationality.

Long-Term Stays and Special Purposes

For travelers planning to stay in Kos for longer than 90 days, or those coming for work, study, or other special purposes, different visa types are required:

Work Visa: Required for those seeking employment in Greece. You will need a job offer and an employer willing to sponsor your visa.

Student Visa: If you plan to study in Greece for more than 90 days, a student visa is required. You must provide proof of admission to a Greek educational institution and show sufficient funds for your stay.

Residence Permit: For those planning to stay long-term or live in Greece, a residence permit is necessary. This permit can be obtained once you're in Greece, but you'll need to meet specific requirements depending on your reason for staying (e.g., work, retirement, family reunification).

Digital Nomad Visa: Greece has introduced a special visa for remote workers. The Digital Nomad Visa allows non-EU citizens to live in Greece while working remotely for an employer based abroad. This can be an excellent option for those who want to experience Greek island life while working online.

Currency and money tips

Official Currency

The official currency used in Kos, as in the rest of Greece, is the Euro (€). Banknotes come in denominations of €5, €10, €20, €50, €100, €200, and €500, while coins range from 1 cent to 2 euros. Travelers coming from outside the Eurozone will need to exchange their local currency for euros upon arrival or before departing for Kos.

Currency Exchange

Banks: Banks in Kos provide currency exchange services, and you'll find branches in most towns, particularly in Kos Town. Banking hours are usually Monday to Friday, from 8:00 AM to 2:00 PM. Keep in mind that banks often offer more favorable exchange rates than currency exchange offices.

Currency Exchange Offices: You'll find dedicated currency exchange offices, particularly in Kos Town, the airport, and around popular tourist areas. These offices are often open for longer hours than banks but may charge higher fees or offer less favorable rates, so it's a good idea to compare options.

ATMs: ATMs are widely available throughout the island, especially in main towns and tourist areas. Most ATMs offer the option to withdraw euros using foreign bank cards. Be aware of potential fees for international transactions and currency conversion, which depend on your home bank. It's wise to inform your bank in advance about your travel plans to avoid any issues with card usage.

Credit Card Acceptance

Credit and debit cards are widely accepted in Kos, particularly in tourist areas, restaurants, hotels, and shops. Visa and MasterCard are the most commonly accepted, though some places may also take American Express. While card usage is convenient, some smaller family-run tavernas, shops, and accommodations may prefer cash, so it's always a good idea to carry some euros with you for smaller transactions or in more remote areas.

Using Cash, Cards, and Traveler's Checks

Cash: It's generally advisable to have some cash on hand, especially for smaller purchases, tipping, and areas where credit cards might not be accepted. Many local markets, small shops, and cafes prefer cash transactions. ATMs are the easiest way to access cash when you need it, but note that there may be withdrawal limits or fees associated with international transactions.

Credit and Debit Cards: As mentioned, credit and debit cards are widely accepted, but be mindful of potential foreign transaction fees charged by your home bank. It's best to check with your bank regarding any fees or restrictions before you travel.

Traveler's Checks: Traveler's checks are becoming less common, and they may not be widely accepted in Kos. If you do choose to bring them, they can usually be cashed at banks, but you'll often need to pay a fee and provide identification. Most travelers find it easier to use ATMs or credit cards instead.

Tipping and Financial Customs

In Kos, tipping is appreciated but not always expected. However, it is customary to leave a small tip in restaurants, cafes, or for taxi drivers if you've received good service.

Restaurants: A typical tip is around 5-10% of the bill. While service is often included in the price, a small extra tip is always appreciated.

Cafes: For coffee or light snacks, rounding up the bill or leaving a euro or two is common.

Taxis: While taxi drivers don't expect a large tip, rounding up the fare or adding €1-2 is standard.

Health and safety information

Vaccinations and Medications

Travelers to Kos do not need any special vaccinations beyond the routine vaccinations recommended for most international travel. However, it's always a good idea to make sure you're up to date on standard vaccinations, including:

- Tetanus
- Measles-Mumps-Rubella (MMR)
- Hepatitis A and B

If you have a specific health condition or are concerned about particular risks, it's worth consulting with a healthcare provider before your trip. For longer stays or travelers venturing into rural areas, it may be worth discussing rabies or tick-borne disease precautions, though these are generally rare concerns for most visitors to Kos.

Local Healthcare Options

Kos has a good healthcare infrastructure to support travelers in case of illness or injury, including hospitals, medical centers, and pharmacies.

Hospitals: The main public hospital is the General Hospital of Kos, located in Kos Town. It provides emergency care and general medical services. For more specialized care, you may need to be transferred to larger hospitals in Athens or Rhodes.

Medical Centers: There are several smaller medical centers and private clinics scattered across the island, particularly in tourist hubs like Kardamena and Kefalos. Many doctors speak English, especially in tourist areas.

Pharmacies: Pharmacies (or "φαρμακείο") are widespread across the island and are often open late. They are a reliable source for over-the-counter medications, basic first aid supplies, and professional advice. Many pharmacists in Kos speak English and can help with minor health concerns.

Emergency Services and Contact Numbers

In case of emergency, Greece has a reliable set of emergency services that can be easily accessed throughout Kos. The most important numbers to know are:

Emergency Number (Police, Fire, Ambulance): 112 – This is the EU-wide emergency number and can be dialed for any kind of urgent assistance.

Ambulance Service: 166

Police (General Assistance): 100

Coast Guard (for sea emergencies): 108

Safety Tips

Beaches and Water Activities

Kos's beaches are generally safe, but it's always good to follow basic safety measures when enjoying the water:

Lifeguards: Many of the popular beaches, such as Paradise Beach and Tigaki Beach, have lifeguards on duty during peak hours. Always swim in designated areas, especially if flags are posted for water conditions.

Currents and Waves: While most beaches have calm waters, always check for warning flags and be cautious if swimming where there are strong currents or waves.

Sun Protection: The Greek sun can be intense, so be sure to use sunscreen, wear a hat, and stay hydrated to avoid heatstroke.

Jellyfish and Sea Urchins: Occasionally, jellyfish or sea urchins may appear near the shore. Wearing water shoes can help prevent injury from stepping on a sea urchin.

Road Travel and Transportation

Road safety is an important consideration, particularly if you plan on renting a car, scooter, or ATV.

Driving: Greeks drive on the right side of the road, and the driving style can be a bit fast-paced. Always follow speed limits, wear your seatbelt, and avoid distractions while driving. Be especially careful on winding mountain roads.

Scooters and ATVs: Many tourists rent scooters or ATVs to get around, but it's essential to wear a helmet and understand local traffic laws. Roads can be narrow and busy during peak season.

Public Transportation: Buses in Kos are generally safe and reliable. Stick to marked bus stops and always keep an eye on your belongings.

Crime Prevention and Personal Safety

Kos is a safe island with a low crime rate, but as with any tourist destination, it's important to stay alert:

Pickpocketing: Be cautious in crowded areas, such as busy streets, markets, or public transport. Keep your belongings secure, and avoid carrying large amounts of cash.

Safe Areas: Kos is known for being a peaceful island, and most areas are safe to walk around at night. Still, it's a good idea to stay in well-lit areas and avoid isolated places, particularly late at night.

Hotel Safes: Use the hotel safe for valuables like passports, credit cards, and expensive electronics.

Natural Disasters and Weather Conditions Kos is generally free from extreme natural disasters, but travelers should still be aware of the following:

Earthquakes: Greece is located in a seismically active region, and minor earthquakes are not uncommon. If an earthquake occurs, seek shelter under sturdy furniture and move away from windows until it passes.

Heatwaves: Summers in Kos can get very hot, with temperatures occasionally exceeding 40°C (104°F). Stay hydrated, avoid strenuous activities during the hottest part of the day, and seek shade when necessary.

Wildfires: Dry summers can sometimes lead to wildfires. Always be aware of local fire warnings and avoid lighting fires or barbecues in dry, wooded areas.

Language tips and basic phrases

The official language spoken in Kos is Greek. While many locals, particularly those in tourist areas, speak English fluently, knowing a few basic Greek phrases can greatly enhance your experience and help you connect with the local culture. Greeks appreciate the effort when visitors try to speak their language, even if it's just a few words.

Common Phrases

Greetings and Introductions:

- Hello: Γειά σας (Yia sas) – Formal / Γειά σου (Yia sou) – Informal
- Good morning: Καλημέρα (Kaliméra)
- Good evening: Καλησπέρα (Kalispéra)
- Good night: Καληνύχτα (Kaliníhta)
- Goodbye: Αντίο (Adío) – More formal / Τα λέμε (Ta léme) – Informal, meaning "see you"
- Please: Παρακαλώ (Parakaló)
- Thank you: Ευχαριστώ (Efharistó)
- You're welcome: Παρακαλώ (Parakaló)
- Yes: Ναι (Ne)
- No: Όχι (Óhi)
- My name is…: Με λένε… (Me léne…)
- Nice to meet you: Χάρηκα (Hárika)

Basic Interactions:

- How much does it cost?: Πόσο κοστίζει; (Póso kostízei?)
- Do you speak English?: Μιλάτε Αγγλικά; (Miláte Angliká?)
- I don't understand: Δεν καταλαβαίνω (Den katalavéno)
- Where is...?: Πού είναι...; (Poú íne...?)
- The bathroom: Η τουαλέτα (Ee toualéta)
- The hotel: Το ξενοδοχείο (To xenodohío)
- The beach: Η παραλία (Ee paralía)
- Water: Νερό (Neró)
- Food: Φαγητό (Faghtó)
- I would like...: Θα ήθελα... (Tha íthela...)
- The bill, please: Τον λογαριασμό, παρακαλώ (Ton logariasmó, parakaló)

Emergency Situations:

- Help!: Βοήθεια! (Voíthia!)
- Call the police: Καλέστε την αστυνομία (Kaléste tin astinomía)
- I need a doctor: Χρειάζομαι γιατρό (Hriázome yatró)
- Is there a pharmacy nearby?: Υπάρχει φαρμακείο εδώ κοντά; (Ipárhi farmakío edó kondá?)
- I am lost: Έχω χαθεί (Ého hathí)

Tips for Communicating with Locals

Pronunciation Guidance: "G" Sound: In Greek, the "g" sound is often soft, like in the English word "yoga." For example, "γειά" (yia) is pronounced more like "ya."

Accents: Pay attention to where the accents fall in Greek words, as they indicate which syllable to emphasize. For instance, in "Καλημέρα" (Kaliméra), the emphasis is on the "mé" syllable.

"Ef" and "Af" Sounds: The letters "ευ" (eu) can be pronounced as either "ef" or "af" depending on the word, like in "Ευχαριστώ" (Efharistó) which is pronounced "ef-ha-ree-STO."

Useful Words and Expressions: Yes is "Ναι" (Ne), which can confuse English speakers who associate "Ne" with "No." Remember, "Ναι" means "yes."

Greek Hospitality: If you hear "καλώς ήρθατε" (kalós írthate), it means "welcome," and it's a sign of Greek hospitality, especially in restaurants or hotels.

Politeness: Using "please" (Παρακαλώ) and "thank you" (Ευχαριστώ) is valued, and politeness goes a long way when interacting with locals.

Cultural Insights for Effective Communication:

Body Language: Greeks are expressive speakers and often use hand gestures to accompany their speech. Don't be surprised by animated conversations!

Nodding and Shaking Your Head: In Greece, nodding can sometimes mean "no," and tilting your head to the side can mean "yes." Pay close attention to both words and gestures.

Directness: Greeks tend to be direct, especially in casual conversations. Don't be taken aback if locals speak frankly; it's part of the culture and not meant to be impolite.

Hospitality and Connection: Even if many people in Kos speak English, attempting to use a few Greek phrases will often result in smiles and warmer interactions. Greeks value personal connections, and even small efforts to speak the language can lead to more authentic experiences.

Climate and best times to visit

Kos enjoys a typical Mediterranean climate, which means long, hot summers and mild, wet winters. The island benefits from over 300 days of sunshine per year, making it a popular destination for sun-seekers. The warm temperatures and favorable weather conditions make it an ideal location for beach holidays, outdoor activities, and exploring the island's rich history year-round.

Seasonal Weather Conditions

Spring (March to May): Spring is one of the most pleasant times to visit Kos. Temperatures range from 15°C to 25°C (59°F to 77°F), with plenty of sunshine and mild evenings. The landscape is lush and green after the winter rains, and flowers are in bloom, making it an ideal time for hiking and sightseeing. Beaches are less crowded, though the sea may still be cool for swimming, especially in early spring.

Summer (June to August): Summer is peak tourist season in Kos, with hot and dry weather. Average daytime temperatures range from 25°C to 35°C (77°F to 95°F), but it can occasionally reach higher in July and August. Evenings are warm, making it perfect for outdoor dining and late-night activities. The sea is warm, and this is the best time for beach lovers and water sports enthusiasts. However, beaches and popular tourist spots can become crowded, especially in July and August.

Autumn (September to November): Autumn is another great time to visit Kos, with pleasant temperatures ranging from 20°C to 30°C (68°F to 86°F) in September and cooling down to 15°C to 20°C (59°F to 68°F) by November. The sea remains warm from the summer heat, making early autumn ideal for swimming and water activities. Tourist crowds begin to thin out, and the island feels more relaxed. October can see occasional rain, but it's still largely sunny.

Winter (December to February): Winter in Kos is mild, with average temperatures between 10°C and 15°C (50°F to 59°F). It's the rainiest season, but there are still plenty of sunny days. While it's too cool for beach activities, winter is a great time for cultural exploration, visiting historical sites, and enjoying the island's quieter atmosphere. Many tourist facilities, including some hotels and restaurants, may close in the winter months, especially in more remote areas.

Best Times to Visit Kos

For Weather and Temperature

The best time to visit Kos for warm weather, beach life, and outdoor activities is from May to October, when the days are long and sunny, and the sea is perfect for swimming. June and September offer the perfect balance of great weather and fewer crowds.

For Tourist Season and Crowds

July and August are the busiest months, when Kos sees an influx of visitors from across Europe. While these months are great for experiencing the island's livelier atmosphere, those seeking a more peaceful experience might prefer May, June, or September, when the weather is still beautiful but without the peak-season crowds.

For Events and Festivals

Kos hosts several cultural and local events throughout the year. The Kos Hippocrates Festival runs through the summer months, celebrating the island's rich cultural heritage with music, performances, and local crafts. For a more traditional experience, visit during the Zia Village Summer Festival or Religious Feast Days in August, which offer a glimpse into local life and celebrations.

For Outdoor Activities and Beach Life

Beach enthusiasts should aim for June through September, when the sea is warm, and all beach services and water sports are available. Spring and autumn are ideal for those interested in hiking, cycling, and exploring the island's natural beauty, with mild temperatures and fewer tourists.

Packing Tips

Summer: Pack light, breathable clothing, sunblock, a wide-brimmed hat, sunglasses, and swimwear. Evenings are warm, but a light jacket or shawl may be useful for breezy nights by the sea.

Spring/Autumn: Layered clothing is recommended, as mornings and evenings can be cooler. Comfortable walking shoes are essential for exploring the island's villages and ancient ruins.

Winter: While winter is mild, pack a warm jacket, umbrella, and waterproof shoes, as you might encounter some rainy days.

Transportation on the island

Kos offers a variety of transportation options, making it easy for travelers to explore the island's towns, beaches, and historic sites. Whether you prefer the flexibility of renting a car or using the island's public transport, there's a suitable option for every type of visitor.

Car Rentals

Renting a car is one of the most popular and convenient ways to explore Kos, especially if you want to visit more remote areas or discover the island at your own pace.

Companies and Locations: You'll find both international and local car rental companies in Kos, with branches at Kos International Airport, Kos Town, and in major tourist areas like Kardamena and Tigaki. Major international companies like Avis, Hertz, Budget, and Enterprise operate on the island, along with several reliable local agencies, such as Kosmos Rent a Car and Autotour Kos.

Types of Vehicles Available: Rental agencies offer a wide range of vehicles, from compact cars ideal for solo travelers or couples to larger SUVs or minivans for families or groups. ATVs and scooters are also popular choices for navigating the island's narrow roads and reaching secluded beaches. Keep in mind that automatic cars are less common, so you may need to request one in advance if you're not comfortable driving a manual transmission.

Public Buses

The public bus system in Kos is well-organized and a great option for budget-conscious travelers who prefer not to rent a car. The bus network, operated by KTEL Kos, connects Kos Town with other major towns, villages, and beaches.

Routes and Schedules: Buses frequently run between Kos Town, Kardamena, Tigaki, Kefalos, Marmari, and other popular destinations. There are also routes to major attractions, such as Asklepion and Paradise Beach. During the high season (summer months), buses run more frequently, especially on the main tourist routes.

Ticket Information: Tickets can be purchased directly from the bus driver or at designated ticket offices in Kos Town. Prices are affordable, typically ranging from €1.50 to €4 depending on the route. For example, a bus ride from Kos Town to Tigaki costs around €2, while a trip to Kefalos might be closer to €4.

Taxis

Taxis are readily available across Kos, particularly in tourist areas and major towns. They're a good option for short trips or if you prefer more direct transport.

Availability and Pricing: Taxis can be found at taxi stands in Kos Town, Kardamena, Mastichari, and near popular attractions. You can also call for a taxi or use local apps. Prices vary based on distance, but a ride from Kos Airport to Kos Town typically costs around €35-€45, while shorter trips within towns may cost around €10-15.

Tips: Most taxis in Kos are metered, but it's a good idea to confirm the fare with the driver before starting your journey, especially for longer trips. Tipping is not mandatory, but rounding up the fare or adding €1-2 is appreciated.

Other Transportation Options

Bicycles: Kos is known for being a bike-friendly island, and many visitors choose to rent bicycles to get around, especially in Kos Town and along the coastline. There are designated bike paths in parts of Kos Town and routes leading to Lambi Beach. Many rental shops across the island offer daily or weekly bicycle rentals for around €5-10 per day.

Scooters and ATVs: Scooters and all-terrain vehicles (ATVs) are widely available for rent. Scooters are a popular option for zipping around the island, especially in smaller towns. ATVs are ideal for more rugged terrain and beach-hopping. Rentals typically cost between €15-30 per day for scooters and €30-50 per day for ATVs. Remember that helmets are mandatory for both, and you will need an international driver's license to rent these vehicles.

Water Taxis: Water taxis connect various beaches and nearby islands. For example, you can take a water taxi from Kos Town to Pserimos or Kalymnos for day trips. Prices vary based on the destination, and schedules are usually posted at the harbor.

Tips for Getting Around the Island

Road Conditions and Driving Tips: The main roads in Kos are generally in good condition, especially along the coast and connecting major towns. However, some smaller roads, particularly in rural or mountainous areas, can be narrow and winding. Drive cautiously and keep an eye out for local drivers, as they may take corners at speed. Gas stations are plentiful, but it's a good idea to fill up before heading to more remote areas.

Parking and Traffic: Parking is relatively easy to find in Kos Town and most tourist areas, with designated parking lots and street parking available. Be mindful of parking restrictions in town centers, particularly during busy summer months. Traffic can increase in peak season, especially around popular beaches and Kos Town, but it is generally not overwhelming.

Using Public Transportation: Buses are an affordable and efficient way to travel between towns and popular tourist spots. Make sure to check the schedules in advance, as service to smaller villages or attractions may be less frequent in the off-season. Keep small change on hand for bus tickets, and arrive at bus stops a little early, especially during busy periods.

Cultural etiquette and local customs

When visiting Kos, it's important to understand and respect the local customs and cultural norms. While the island is welcoming and used to tourists, a little cultural sensitivity can go a long way in fostering positive interactions with locals and enhancing your experience.

Social Etiquette

Greetings: In Greece, greetings are typically warm and friendly. When meeting someone for the first time, a simple "Yia sas" (Hello) or "Kaliméra" (Good morning) is customary. Greeks often use a handshake for formal introductions. Among friends, a kiss on both cheeks (left, then right) is common.

When addressing someone older or in a formal setting, it's polite to use "Kyrie" (Mr.) or "Kyria" (Mrs.) followed by their last name.

Body Language: Greeks are expressive and often use hand gestures in conversation. One gesture to avoid is showing your palm with fingers extended, as this can be seen as rude. Instead, if you need to signal "stop" or "no," a more subtle gesture is recommended. Eye contact is important in conversations, as it conveys trust and sincerity.

Personal Space: While Greeks tend to stand closer than people from some other cultures, especially during conversations, respect personal space in more formal settings. It's common for locals to show warmth through gestures like touching your arm or shoulder during a conversation.

Dining Customs

Mealtimes: Greeks enjoy a relaxed approach to meals. Lunch, the main meal of the day, is typically served between 2:00 PM and 3:00 PM, while dinner starts late, often around 8:00 PM to 10:00 PM. Greeks enjoy long, leisurely meals, often shared with family and friends.

Table Manners: When dining at a taverna, it's polite to wait until everyone is served before beginning to eat. Sharing dishes is common in Greek culture, so expect to pass around plates of meze (small dishes). Always compliment the host or chef with a simple "Efharistó" (Thank you) if you're dining in someone's home.

At the end of a meal, it's typical to receive complimentary fruit or dessert, such as watermelon or yogurt with honey.

Traditional Cuisine: Kos offers a variety of traditional dishes like moussaka, souvlaki, and fresh seafood. Try local specialties, including pitaridia (homemade pasta) and posa cheese (a unique cheese preserved in red wine). Bread is served with almost every meal, and it's common to use it to scoop up food or sauces.

Religious and Cultural Sites

Dress Code: When visiting religious sites such as churches or monasteries, modest dress is required. Visitors should cover their shoulders and avoid wearing shorts or short skirts. Women may be asked to wear a headscarf, though this is not always required.

It's respectful to keep voices low, refrain from using flash photography, and avoid walking in front of people praying.

Behavior: When entering a Greek Orthodox church, it's customary to make the sign of the cross (though this is not required for visitors). During religious services, it's polite to stand quietly at the back if you're not participating. Always ask before taking photos inside churches or sacred spaces, as some may prohibit photography.

Local Festivals and Events

Participation: Festivals are a big part of Greek culture, and Kos hosts several events throughout the year. The Kos Hippocrates Festival in the summer, for instance, celebrates the island's rich history and includes music, performances, and art exhibitions. Visitors are welcome to join in the celebrations, but it's important to behave respectfully, particularly during religious festivals like Easter.

Etiquette: When attending a festival, follow the locals' lead. Dress appropriately for the occasion, and be mindful of religious processions or ceremonies. It's common to be offered food or drink during celebrations—accepting hospitality is a sign of respect and appreciation.

Tips: Be aware that festivals and events can attract large crowds. Arriving early is a good idea if you want to secure a spot, and it's always polite to thank locals for their hospitality.

Everyday Interactions

Shopping: In most stores in Kos, prices are fixed, but at markets or smaller shops, there's some room for bargaining, particularly for items like souvenirs or crafts. However, bargaining should be done respectfully and with a friendly attitude—locals enjoy a good-humored exchange.

Tipping: While tipping is not mandatory, it is appreciated, especially in tourist areas. In restaurants, it's customary to leave a tip of around 5-10% of the bill. If you've received excellent service, rounding up the bill or adding a few euros as a tip is a nice gesture.

For taxi drivers, rounding up the fare to the nearest euro is common. Tipping hotel staff (such as porters or cleaners) with €1-2 for their service is also appreciated.

Hospitality: Greeks are known for their hospitality, or philoxenia (love of strangers). If you're invited into someone's home or offered something, it's polite to accept, even if just a small amount. Refusing hospitality can be seen as impolite, so a simple "Efharistó" (Thank you) with a smile goes a long way.

Find Your Way with QR Codes

We've added QR codes throughout this guide to make navigating easier. Here's how to use them:

1. Scan the QR Code using your smartphone's camera or a QR code scanner app.
2. Open in a Browser (like Chrome, Safari, or Firefox) when prompted, instead of the Google Maps app, for the best results.
3. View the Destination on the Google Maps page that opens. You'll find useful details like photos and reviews.
4. Tap "Directions" to get step-by-step guidance from your current location.
5. Follow the Route provided by Google Maps and enjoy your trip!

Remember to choose a browser to avoid any issues. Safe travels!

Accommodation Options

Luxury Hotels

Lango Design Hotel & Spa

Lango Design Hotel & Spa is an adults-only retreat offering contemporary luxury in a serene beachfront setting near Lambi Beach. Known for its sleek, modern architecture and artistic decor, this boutique hotel is ideal for couples or honeymooners seeking tranquility. The hotel offers a range of spacious rooms and suites, many with private pools or sea views, equipped with luxury amenities like king-size beds and Nespresso machines. Dining options include Mediterranean cuisine at the on-site restaurant, and the spa offers treatments such as massages and hammam experiences. Located just a short drive from Kos Town, Lango provides easy access to key attractions like Nerantzia Castle.

Price Range: €200-€500 per night.

Diamond Deluxe Hotel

Diamond Deluxe Hotel is a five-star, adults-only property renowned for its glamorous, all-white design and expansive pool complex. Guests can choose from double rooms, suites with private pools, or luxury villas, all featuring jacuzzis and private terraces. The hotel's Emerald Restaurant serves Mediterranean gourmet cuisine, and the Mazarin Spa offers holistic treatments, including hydrotherapy and steam rooms. Located near Lambi Beach and a short distance from Kos Town, the hotel is conveniently close to attractions like the Roman Odeon and Casa Romana.

Price Range: €250-€600 per night.

Michelangelo Resort & Spa

Michelangelo Resort & Spa is perched on a cliff in Agios Fokas, offering stunning panoramic views of the Aegean. Known for its infinity pools and luxurious design, this five-star resort is perfect for relaxation. Accommodations include classic rooms, superior rooms, and executive suites, all featuring luxury amenities like marble bathrooms and

espresso machines. The resort boasts multiple dining options and the Therme Spa, which offers massages, hydrotherapy, and body wraps. Close to attractions like Therma Beach, Michelangelo is a 10-minute drive from Kos Town.
Price Range: €300-€700 per night.

Mitsis Blue Domes Resort & Spa

Mitsis Blue Domes is a luxurious beachfront resort in Kardamena, combining traditional Greek architecture with modern luxury. The resort offers bungalows, family suites, and villas with private pools, featuring direct beach access and modern amenities. With over ten dining options, including Greek, Italian, and Asian cuisines, guests are spoilt for choice. The Blue Domes Spa provides a variety of treatments, including aromatherapy massages and facials. The resort is close to popular beaches and attractions like Antimachia Castle, with Kos International Airport just a 15-minute drive away.
Price Range: €350-€800 per night.

Astir Odysseus Kos Resort & Spa

Astir Odysseus is a luxury beachfront resort located near Tigaki Beach, offering a peaceful escape with its spacious gardens and beachfront pools. Accommodation options range from standard rooms to maisonettes, many with private pools or jacuzzis. Guests can enjoy dining at several on-site restaurants, including the Achilles Buffet and Argo Beach Tavern, serving Greek and international dishes. The Aegeo Spa offers a full range of treatments, from massages to steam baths. The resort is a 15-minute drive from Kos Town, close to attractions like the Asklepion and Ancient Agora.

Price Range: €400-€900 per night.

White Rock of Kos

White Rock of Kos is a five-star, adults-only boutique hotel situated on the hills above Kefalos, offering breathtaking views of the Aegean. Known for its privacy and luxury, the hotel features spacious suites, many with private pools or hot tubs, and each offering panoramic sea views. Amenities include modern furnishings, rain showers, and private terraces. Guests can enjoy Mediterranean cuisine at the hotel's restaurant, relax at the poolside bar, or unwind with treatments at the spa. The hotel's secluded location offers peace and quiet while still being a short drive from Kefalos Beach and the island's top attractions.

Price Range: €300-€700 per night.

Grecotel Luxme Kos Imperial

Grecotel Luxme Kos Imperial is a sprawling beachfront resort located near Psalidi Beach, known for its lush gardens, lagoon-style pools, and family-friendly atmosphere. The hotel offers a variety of rooms, suites, and bungalows, many with sea views or private pools. Guests can enjoy multiple dining options, from Greek and Mediterranean cuisine to international flavors, and the hotel's Elixir Spa offers wellness treatments, including massages and facials. With facilities like a kids' club, water sports, and tennis courts, it's perfect for families and couples alike.

Price Range: €250-€600 per night.

OKU Kos

OKU Kos is a stylish, adults-only beachfront retreat that combines minimalist design with a laid-back atmosphere. The hotel features a collection of suites and villas, all with private terraces or gardens, and some with private pools. The neutral, earthy tones and natural materials used in the decor create a sense of calm and tranquility. OKU Kos is known for its farm-to-table dining experience, offering locally sourced ingredients in its restaurant. The hotel's wellness area includes a spa, yoga pavilion, and a fitness center. Located near Marmari Beach, it offers both seclusion and easy access to nearby attractions.

Price Range: €300-€750 per night.

Kyma Rooms & Suites

Kyma Rooms & Suites is a boutique hotel located in Kos Town, offering modern, stylish accommodations with a focus on comfort and convenience. The rooms and suites are elegantly furnished, with amenities such as private balconies, sea views, and rainfall showers. The hotel is within walking distance of the town's vibrant nightlife, restaurants, and cultural attractions, such as the Ancient Agora and Nerantzia Castle. Although smaller in scale than the island's resorts, Kyma offers personalized service and a more intimate setting for travelers seeking a central location.

Price Range: €150-€400 per night.

Cabana Blu Hotel & Suites

Cabana Blu Hotel & Suites is a luxurious, modern hotel located in Kardamena, offering a mix of suites and villas, many with private pools or sea views. The hotel blends modern design with Mediterranean influences, and its rooms are equipped with high-end amenities like king-size beds, private terraces, and spacious living areas. Guests can enjoy Mediterranean and international cuisine at the on-site restaurant, as well as a variety of cocktails at the pool bar.

The hotel's location near Kardamena Beach and its proximity to Antimachia Castle make it an ideal base for both relaxation and exploration.

Price Range: €250-€600 per night.

Aqua Blu Boutique Hotel + Spa

Aqua Blu Boutique Hotel + Spa is an adults-only, five-star hotel located near Lambi Beach. Known for its chic, contemporary design, this boutique hotel offers luxurious suites, many with private pools and sea views. The Cuvée Restaurant is one of the highlights, serving gourmet cuisine with a focus on fresh, local ingredients. The hotel's Tamaris Spa offers a wide range of wellness treatments, including massages, facials, and a hammam. Located close to Kos Town, Aqua Blu provides easy access to local attractions while offering a peaceful retreat for guests.

Price Range: €300-€700 per night.

Mid-Range Hotels

Hotel Esperia

Hotel Esperia is a well-located mid-range hotel in the heart of Marmari, offering comfortable accommodations and a friendly atmosphere. The hotel features standard rooms and family rooms, all equipped with balconies, air conditioning, and modern amenities. Guests can relax by the outdoor pool, enjoy drinks at the poolside bar, or dine at the on-site restaurant, which serves both local and international cuisine. The hotel is just a short walk from Marmari Beach, making it a great option for travelers looking for affordable yet convenient accommodations near the sea.

Price Range: €60-€120 per night.

Alexandra Beach Hotel

Located near Psalidi Beach, Alexandra Beach Hotel offers modern, comfortable accommodations with beautiful views of the Aegean Sea. The hotel features a variety of room types, including double rooms and family suites, many with sea-view balconies. Guests can enjoy the outdoor pool, restaurant, and bar, with easy access to the beach just a short walk away. The hotel is also a short drive from Kos Town, making it a great base for exploring the island's attractions, including the Asklepion and Therma Beach.

Price Range: €70-€150 per night.

Kos Bay Hotel

Kos Bay Hotel is a budget-friendly, mid-range hotel located in Kos Town, offering simple yet comfortable rooms, many with balconies overlooking the marina. The hotel provides easy access to the town's shops, restaurants, and cultural attractions, such as Nerantzia Castle and the Ancient Agora. Guests can enjoy a continental breakfast and relax at the hotel bar. Its convenient location makes it a popular choice for travelers looking to explore Kos Town on foot.

Price Range: €50-€100 per night.

TUI Suneo Niriides Beach

TUI Suneo Niriides Beach is a family-friendly hotel located near Psalidi Beach, offering comfortable accommodations with a focus on all-inclusive service. The hotel features standard rooms and family suites, each equipped with modern amenities and balconies. Guests can enjoy multiple pools, a buffet restaurant serving Mediterranean and international cuisine, and organized activities for children and adults alike. The hotel's location near Psalidi Beach and its proximity to Kos Town make it ideal for both beach lovers and those looking to explore the local culture.

Price Range: €80-€160 per night.

Cleopatra Classic Hotel

Cleopatra Classic Hotel is a popular mid-range option in Kardamena, known for its welcoming atmosphere and central location. The hotel offers a variety of room types, including family rooms, all with air conditioning and private balconies. Guests can relax by the outdoor pool, enjoy drinks at the bar, or explore the nearby shops, restaurants, and nightlife in Kardamena. The hotel is a short walk from

Kardamena Beach and within easy reach of attractions like Antimachia Castle.

Price Range: €60-€140 per night.

Budget Hotels

Theros All Suite Hotel - Adults Only

Theros All Suite Hotel is a chic, adults-only boutique hotel located near Lambi Beach, offering an affordable yet luxurious stay. The hotel features modern suites, each with minimalist decor, private balconies, and premium amenities. Guests can enjoy the outdoor pool and relax at the poolside bar. The hotel's peaceful setting, combined with its proximity to Kos Town, makes it an excellent choice for couples looking for a quiet retreat.

Price Range: €80-€150 per night.

KoSea Boutique Hotel

KoSea Boutique Hotel, located in Kos Town, is a stylish budget option that offers a blend of modern design and comfort. Rooms and suites come with contemporary furnishings, air conditioning, and balconies. The hotel features a large outdoor pool, a sun terrace, and an on-site restaurant serving Mediterranean dishes. Its central location allows guests to explore the nearby beaches and cultural attractions with ease, including Kos Marina and the Roman Odeon.

Price Range: €60-€130 per night.

Kosta Palace

Kosta Palace is a well-known budget hotel located in Kos Town, right on the waterfront, offering fantastic views of the medieval Nerantzia Castle and the harbor. The hotel offers simple, comfortable rooms and apartments with kitchenettes, making it ideal for families or longer stays. Guests can relax by the rooftop pool or enjoy a drink at the bar while overlooking the marina. Its central location puts it within easy reach of shops, restaurants, and the ferry terminal.

Price Range: €50-€110 per night.

Blue Lagoon City Hotel

Blue Lagoon City Hotel is a budget-friendly option located in Kos Town, part of the well-known Blue Lagoon hotel chain. The hotel offers clean, modern rooms with private balconies and comfortable amenities. Guests can enjoy the indoor and outdoor pools, a fitness center, and the on-site restaurant. Its central location provides easy access to Kos Town's lively bars, restaurants, and historical landmarks such as the Ancient Agora and Hippocrates Tree.

Price Range: €70-€140 per night.

Chapter 3: Must-See Attractions

Asklepion

Address: Asklepion, 4 km southwest of Kos Town, Kos 85300

What to Expect: The Asklepion is an ancient healing temple dedicated to Asclepius, the Greek god of medicine. Visitors can explore the ruins of the complex, including its temples, healing chambers, and ancient medical centers. The site is spread across several terraces, connected by stone steps, offering stunning views of the surrounding hills and coastline. Informative plaques and signs provide details about the history of the site and the treatments that took place here.

What to Bring: Wear comfortable shoes for walking across uneven terrain, and bring water and sunscreen, as the site is open and there is limited shade. A hat and sunglasses are also recommended during summer months.

Price: €8 per adult, €4 for reduced admission (students, seniors). Children under 18 can enter for free.

The Basilica of Agios Stefanos

Address: Kefalos, Kos 85301 (near Agios Stefanos Beach)

What to Expect: The Basilica of Agios Stefanos is a picturesque ruin of an early Christian basilica overlooking the sea. The remains include sections of two basilicas built in the 5th and 6th centuries AD, featuring columns, mosaics, and part of the apse. The location, right by the beach, offers great views of Kastri Islet, with its iconic white chapel. Visitors can freely walk through the ruins and admire the view.

What to Bring: Comfortable footwear for walking over uneven ground and swimwear if you plan to visit the nearby beach. Sunscreen, water, and a hat are also advisable.

Price: Free entry.

Casa Romana Kos

Address: Casa Romana, Grigoriou E 16, Kos Town 85300

What to Expect: Casa Romana is a beautifully restored Roman villa dating back to the 3rd century AD. The villa gives a glimpse into Roman life with its many rooms, atriums, and intricate mosaic floors. Visitors can explore the well-preserved courtyards and fountains, as well as admire restored artifacts from the period. The villa's layout and mosaics are impressive, making it one of the most important Roman sites in Kos Town.

What to Bring: Light clothing, as you'll be walking through the villa and its open courtyards. A camera is recommended for capturing the detailed mosaics. There is little shade, so sunscreen and a hat are useful, especially in the summer.

Price: €6 per adult, €3 for reduced admission (students, seniors), and free entry for children under 18.

Roman Odeon of Kos

Address: Roman Odeon, Leoforos Grigoriou V, Kos Town 85300

What to Expect: The Roman Odeon is an ancient amphitheater built in the 2nd century AD. It was used for music performances and political gatherings in Roman times. Visitors can walk through the well-preserved seating area, the orchestra pit, and the stage. The site also offers glimpses into the underground chambers where gladiators and performers once prepared. Informative signs explain the structure and history of the Odeon.

What to Bring: Comfortable shoes, as the steps and seating areas are made of stone. It's a good idea to bring water, especially in the summer months. A camera is a must to capture the historical ambiance.

Price: Free entry.

Nerantzia Castle (Castle of the Knights)

Address: Kos Harbour, Kos Town 85300

What to Expect: Nerantzia Castle, also known as the Castle of the Knights, was built by the Knights of St. John in the 14th century to defend against Ottoman invasions. The castle's massive stone walls, bastions, and towers are well-preserved, offering fantastic views of the Aegean Sea and Kos Town's harbor. Visitors can walk along the fortifications and explore the castle grounds, including its ancient stone bridges and gates.

What to Bring: Comfortable footwear, as there is a lot of walking and climbing involved. Bring water and sunscreen, as much of the site is open to the sun. A camera is essential for the views of the harbor and Kos Town.

Price: €4 per adult, reduced admission for students and seniors at €2, and free for children under 18.

Antimachia Castle

Address: Antimachia, Kos 85302

What to Expect: Antimachia Castle is a medieval fortress located on a hill overlooking the village of Antimachia. Built by the Knights of St. John in the 14th century, the castle offers impressive views of the surrounding countryside and the coast. Visitors can explore the castle ruins, including its outer walls, gates, and remnants of churches within the grounds. The wide open spaces inside the castle give a sense of its historical significance and its role in defending Kos from invasions.

What to Bring: Sturdy shoes for walking on rocky and uneven terrain, as well as water, sunscreen, and a hat, as the castle is exposed to the sun with little shade. A camera is a must for the panoramic views.

Price: Free entry.

Western Archaeological Zone

Address: Leoforos Grigoriou E, Kos Town 85300

What to Expect: The Western Archaeological Zone is one of the most important archaeological areas in Kos, offering visitors a glimpse into the ancient city's layout. The site includes impressive ruins such as Roman baths, mosaics, and the remains of an ancient gymnasium. Visitors can walk along ancient streets and marvel at the well-preserved remnants of Roman houses, public baths, and courtyards. There are also several ancient columns and statues that add to the historical atmosphere.

What to Bring: Comfortable shoes, as the site covers a large area. Sunscreen and water are recommended, as the zone is mostly open-air. Bring a guidebook or download an app for additional historical information as you explore.

Price: Free entry.

Ancient Agora

Address: Kos Town Center, Kos 85300

What to Expect: The Ancient Agora of Kos was once the bustling center of ancient Kos and remains a significant archaeological site. Visitors can explore the ruins of temples, columns, and public buildings that date back to the 3rd century BC. The site includes remains of an early Christian basilica and various sanctuaries dedicated to Greek gods. It's a beautiful area for history enthusiasts and photographers, as it sits near the coastline and offers views of the sea.

What to Bring: Wear comfortable footwear, as the ruins cover a large area. Bring sunscreen, a hat, and water, as there is minimal shade. A camera is essential for capturing the ancient ruins and the sea backdrop.

Price: Free entry.

Hippocrates Tree

Address: Kos Town Center, Kos 85300 (near Nerantzia Castle)

What to Expect: The Hippocrates Tree is a historical landmark located in Kos Town. Legend has it that this ancient tree is where Hippocrates, the father of modern medicine, taught his students. While the current tree is not the original, it is believed to be over 500 years old and is a descendant of the original plane tree. Visitors can sit in the shade of this impressive tree and reflect on the historical significance of Kos as a center of learning and medicine in the ancient world.

What to Bring: A camera to capture the symbolic landmark and its surroundings. Bring water and wear comfortable shoes, as the area is within walking distance of other Kos Town attractions.

Price: Free entry.

Plaka Forest

Address: Plaka, Kos 85301 (near Antimachia)

What to Expect: Plaka Forest is a peaceful pine forest located near Antimachia, known for its natural beauty and its population of peacocks, which roam freely through the trees. Visitors can walk through the shaded forest, have a picnic, and observe the wildlife. It's an excellent spot for families and nature lovers, providing a break from the beach and cultural sites. There are also picnic tables available for a relaxing meal in nature.

What to Bring: Comfortable walking shoes, a picnic basket if you plan to eat, and plenty of water. A camera to capture the wildlife, especially the colorful peacocks.

Price: Free entry.

Chapter 4: Beaches and Water Activities

Paradise Beach

Address: Paradise Beach, Kefalos, Kos 85301

What to Expect: Paradise Beach is one of the most popular beaches on Kos, known for its soft golden sand and crystal-clear waters. The shallow water makes it ideal for swimming, snorkeling, and water sports. Families love this beach for its calm waves, while thrill-seekers can enjoy activities like jet skiing, banana boats, and paddleboarding. The beach is well-serviced, with sunbeds, umbrellas, and several beach bars offering refreshments and snacks.

What to Bring: Sunscreen, towels, swimwear, and cash for renting sunbeds or equipment. Water shoes can be useful for rocky patches near the shore.

Price: Free entry, but expect to pay around €8-€10 for a sunbed and umbrella. Water sports are available for an additional fee.

Kardamena Beach

Address: Kardamena Beach, Kardamena, Kos 85302

What to Expect: Located near the lively town of Kardamena, this long sandy beach is perfect for both relaxation and adventure. Kardamena Beach offers plenty of amenities, including sunbeds, umbrellas, and beachfront tavernas. Water sports are popular here, with options such as windsurfing, water skiing, and parasailing. The nearby town provides a variety of restaurants, bars, and shops, making it a great place to spend the day and enjoy the vibrant atmosphere.

What to Bring: Swimwear, sunscreen, and water sports gear if you plan to take part. Bring cash for food, drinks, and water sports activities.

Price: Free entry, sunbeds cost around €5-€8. Water sports prices vary.

Therma Beach (Embros Therme)

Address: Therma Beach, Agios Fokas, Kos 85300 (8 km from Kos Town)

What to Expect: Therma Beach is famous for its natural hot springs that flow into the sea, creating warm waters along the rocky shore. The natural thermal pools are believed to have healing properties, and many visitors come here to soak in the hot waters. The beach itself is pebbly, and while it lacks the sandy shores of other beaches, its unique setting and therapeutic waters make it a must-visit. The surrounding cliffs add to the dramatic scenery.

What to Bring: Water shoes are highly recommended for walking on the rocky beach and in the hot spring area. Bring towels, swimwear, and water, as there are limited facilities at the beach.

Price: Free entry.

Agios Stefanos Beach

Address: Agios Stefanos Beach, Kefalos, Kos 85301

What to Expect: Agios Stefanos Beach is known for its picturesque ruins of the Basilica of Agios Stefanos, which sit right on the beach. The beach offers clear blue waters and a mix of sand and pebbles, making it perfect for swimming and snorkeling. From the shore, visitors can admire the view of Kastri Islet, a small island with a white chapel that is easily accessible by swimming or paddling. Sunbeds and umbrellas are available for rent, and the beach has a few nearby cafes for refreshments.

What to Bring: Swimwear, sunscreen, and snorkeling gear if you want to explore the waters around Kastri Islet. Bring water and snacks if you plan to spend a long time at the beach.

Price: Free entry, with sunbeds costing around €5-€7.

Tigaki Beach

Address: Tigaki Beach, Tigaki, Kos 85300 (11 km from Kos Town)

What to Expect: Tigaki Beach is a long stretch of white sand with shallow, calm waters, making it ideal for families and those looking for a relaxing day by the sea. The beach is well-organized with plenty of sunbeds and umbrellas for rent. The area is popular for windsurfing and other water sports, and visitors can easily rent equipment from nearby shops. The beachside cafes and tavernas offer local dishes and drinks, making it a great spot for a leisurely lunch.

What to Bring: Sunscreen, towels, and swimwear. Water sports gear is available for rent, but you can bring your own if preferred.

Price: Free entry, with sunbeds available for around €6-€10. Windsurfing and other water activities are available for an additional fee.

Marmari Beach

Address: Marmari Beach, Marmari, Kos 85300

What to Expect: Marmari Beach is a long, sandy beach located on the northern coast of Kos, known for its shallow waters and peaceful atmosphere. It's less crowded than other popular beaches, making it a great spot for families and those seeking relaxation. Marmari Beach is well-organized, with sunbeds, umbrellas, and a few beachfront cafes and tavernas offering food and drinks. The calm, clear waters are perfect for swimming and windsurfing, with equipment available for rent.

What to Bring: Swimwear, sunscreen, towels, and cash for renting sunbeds and buying refreshments. If you're interested in windsurfing, bring gear or rent it on-site.

Price: Free entry, with sunbeds costing around €5-€8.

Agios Fokas Beach (Psalidi)

Address: Agios Fokas Beach, Psalidi, Kos 85300

What to Expect: Located near Therma Beach, Agios Fokas is a pebbly beach that offers a more secluded and tranquil experience. It's known for its darker, volcanic sand and therapeutic properties. The beach is well-organized with sunbeds, umbrellas, and nearby beach bars offering drinks and snacks. The views of the Turkish coast from here are stunning, making it a favorite for visitors seeking both relaxation and scenery. The calm waters also make it a great spot for swimming and snorkeling.

What to Bring: Water shoes for the pebbles, swimwear, sunscreen, and towels. A camera is recommended for capturing the views of the Turkish coastline.

Price: Free entry, with sunbeds costing around €6-€9.

Agios Theologos Beach

Address: Agios Theologos Beach, Kefalos, Kos 85301

What to Expect: Agios Theologos Beach is a remote, wild beach located near Kefalos on the island's western coast. Known for its rugged beauty, dramatic cliffs, and stunning sunsets, it's popular among those seeking solitude and surfers looking to catch some waves. The beach is less developed, so visitors won't find the usual tourist facilities here, but its untouched beauty makes it worth a visit. There is a small taverna near the beach, offering local food and drinks.

What to Bring: Water shoes for walking on the rocky areas, a hat, sunscreen, and water. If you're planning to surf, bring your gear or check ahead for rentals.

Price: Free entry.

Lambi Beach

Address: Lambi Beach, Kos Town, Kos 85300

What to Expect: Located just a short distance from Kos Town, Lambi Beach is a lively and popular spot for both locals and tourists. With soft golden sand and plenty of beach bars, it's a great place for sunbathing, swimming, and enjoying beachside dining. The beach offers sunbeds, umbrellas, and a variety of water sports, such as jet skiing and parasailing. Its proximity to Kos Town means that visitors can easily walk to nearby restaurants and shops after a day at the beach.

What to Bring: Swimwear, sunscreen, towels, and cash for water sports and refreshments. Lambi Beach is great for spending the whole day relaxing, so bring everything you need for a comfortable visit.

Price: Free entry, with sunbeds available for €6-€10.

Chapter 5: Villages and Towns

Zia Village

Zia Village is one of the most beautiful and traditional villages in Kos, located on the slopes of Mount Dikeos. This small mountain village is famous for its breathtaking sunsets, making it a popular spot for photographers and travelers looking for a serene atmosphere. In Zia, you'll find narrow streets lined with local craft shops selling handmade items, olive oil, and herbs. The village is also home to several traditional tavernas offering stunning panoramic views of the island and the Aegean Sea, where you can enjoy local dishes like moussaka and grilled lamb. It's a great place for a leisurely evening stroll, and the nearby hiking trails provide access to the peak of Mount Dikeos for more adventurous visitors.

What to Bring: Comfortable walking shoes, a camera for the sunset, and some cash for local products and dining.

Must-Do: Shop for local crafts and olive oil, and enjoy dinner with sunset views at a hilltop taverna.

Asfendiou Village

Asfendiou is a traditional village situated on the slopes of Mount Dikeos, offering a peaceful retreat from the more crowded tourist areas. Known for its beautiful stone houses and old churches, Asfendiou gives visitors a glimpse into traditional village life on Kos. The village is surrounded by greenery and offers excellent views of the coast and countryside. It’s a great destination for those interested in history and architecture, as many of the buildings have been well-preserved. Asfendiou is also a perfect base for hiking, with trails that lead through the surrounding hills and valleys.

What to Bring: Walking shoes, water, and a camera to capture the scenic views.

Must-Do: Explore the ancient churches, including the Church of Agios Ioannis, and take a hike in the surrounding hills.

Antimachia

Antimachia is a charming village located inland, near Kos International Airport. The village is known for its traditional windmill and the nearby Antimachia Castle, a medieval fortress that offers incredible views over the island and the surrounding sea. Visitors to Antimachia can explore the old windmill, which still operates, and learn about the traditional ways of grinding wheat into flour. The village also has a traditional house museum, where you can see how people in Kos lived in the past. Antimachia is also famous for its honey production, and you can purchase local honey and olive oil from family-run shops.

What to Bring: Comfortable shoes for walking around the village and exploring the castle. Bring cash if you plan to buy honey or visit the local shops.

Must-Do: Visit Antimachia Castle for stunning views, and explore the windmill to see a working piece of Kos's history.

Kardamena

Kardamena is a lively seaside town located on the southern coast of Kos. It's one of the most popular tourist destinations on the island, known for its long sandy beach, vibrant nightlife, and wide range of activities. The beach is well-equipped with sunbeds, umbrellas, and watersports, making it a great place for both relaxation and adventure. Kardamena is also home to numerous restaurants, bars, and shops, giving visitors plenty of options for dining and entertainment. The town's nightlife is one of the best on the island, with a variety of bars and clubs that stay open late into the night.

What to Bring: Swimwear, sunscreen, and cash for food, drinks, and activities.

Must-Do: Spend the day at Kardamena Beach, enjoy watersports, and explore the town's vibrant nightlife.

Kefalos

Kefalos is a picturesque hilltop village located on the western side of Kos. The village offers stunning views of the surrounding coastline and is known for its traditional charm, with whitewashed houses, narrow streets, and beautiful flower-filled courtyards. Kefalos is also close to some of the island's best beaches, including Agios Stefanos Beach and Paradise Beach, making it an ideal location for beachgoers. The village is home to several tavernas serving traditional Greek food, and the nearby Basilica of Agios Stefanos is a must-see for history lovers.

What to Bring: Comfortable shoes for walking around the village, and swimwear if you plan to visit the nearby beaches.

Must-Do: Visit the Basilica of Agios Stefanos, relax on nearby beaches, and enjoy a meal at a local taverna with sea views.

Paleo Pili

Paleo Pili is an ancient, abandoned village located in the mountains, offering visitors a glimpse into the medieval history of Kos. The village was once a thriving community but was abandoned after a major earthquake. Today, visitors can explore the ruins of old houses, churches, and the impressive Pili Castle, which sits atop a hill with panoramic views of the island and the Aegean Sea. The hike up to the castle is challenging but rewarding, and the surrounding landscape is filled with lush greenery and wildlife.

What to Bring: Sturdy shoes for hiking, water, and a camera to capture the views from the top.

Must-Do: Hike to Pili Castle, explore the village ruins, and enjoy the breathtaking views of Kos.

Mylotopi

Mylotopi is a small traditional windmill and folklore museum near Kefalos that offers visitors a chance to learn about the island's rural history. The museum features exhibits on traditional bread-making, farming techniques, and the daily life of past generations on Kos. The restored windmill is still in operation and provides a fascinating look at how wheat was traditionally ground into flour. Visitors can also enjoy beautiful views of the surrounding countryside and coastline from the museum's location.

What to Bring: Comfortable walking shoes and a camera to capture the windmill and surrounding scenery.

Must-Do: Visit the windmill, explore the folklore museum, and take in the views of the Kefalos area.

Nikia Village (Nisyros)

Located on the volcanic island of Nisyros, just a short boat ride from Kos, Nikia Village is a charming mountain village with narrow streets, traditional houses, and stunning views of the island's volcanic caldera. The village is known for its quiet, picturesque atmosphere and is a great place to experience authentic Greek island life. Nikia's small cafes and restaurants offer delicious local dishes, and visitors can explore the village's churches and learn about the island's volcanic history.

What to Bring: Comfortable shoes for walking around the village's hilly streets, and a camera for capturing the caldera views.

Must-Do: Visit the Volcanological Museum, enjoy local food, and take in the views of the volcanic landscape.

Chapter 6: Food and Drink

Traditional Dishes to Try

Kos boasts a variety of traditional dishes that showcase its culinary heritage. Here are some must-try local specialties:

1. **Moussaka**: A signature Greek dish made with layers of eggplant, minced meat (usually lamb or beef), potatoes, and creamy béchamel sauce. This baked casserole is a hearty favorite in Kos.
2. **Souvlaki**: A popular street food, souvlaki consists of skewered, grilled meat (pork or chicken), served with pita bread, tomatoes, onions, and tzatziki. It's perfect for a quick and satisfying meal.
3. **Greek Salad**: A refreshing mix of ripe tomatoes, cucumbers, red onions, feta cheese, and olives, drizzled with olive oil and sprinkled with oregano. This simple yet delicious dish is a staple at every taverna.
4. **Fresh Seafood:** Kos's location in the Aegean means seafood is abundant. Grilled octopus, sea bass, and calamari are must-tries, often served simply with olive oil, lemon, and herbs.
5. **Pitaridia**: Unique to Kos, this homemade pasta is made with flour, water, and salt. It's typically served with a light tomato sauce or meat stew, offering a taste of the island's rustic culinary traditions.

6. **Meze**: A selection of small, shareable dishes that include items like tzatziki, grilled vegetables, saganaki (fried cheese), and dolmades (stuffed grape leaves). Meze is a great way to sample a variety of local flavors in one sitting.

Best Local Tavernas and Restaurants in Kos Town

Taverna Petrino

Located in the heart of Kos Town, Taverna Petrino offers a traditional Greek dining experience with a focus on grilled meats and fresh seafood. The outdoor seating is charming, and the atmosphere is welcoming, making it a favorite for both locals and tourists.

Price Range: €15-€30 per person

Must-Try: Grilled octopus, souvlaki, and moussaka.

Barbouni Seafood Restaurant

Right on the waterfront in Kos Town, Barbouni is known for its excellent seafood and Mediterranean dishes. With views of the harbor, it's a great spot for a leisurely lunch or dinner by the sea. The restaurant prides itself on serving fresh fish, caught daily.

Price Range: €30-€50 per person

Must-Try: Grilled sea bass, seafood pasta, and fried calamari.

Elia

A more contemporary restaurant in Kos Town, Elia offers a modern take on traditional Greek dishes, using seasonal ingredients and innovative presentations. The chic interior and creative menu make it an ideal spot for a more refined dining experience.

Price Range: €20-€40 per person

Must-Try: Seasonal meze, lamb with yogurt sauce, and grilled fish.

Alberto Restaurant

Located along the Kos Town waterfront, Alberto is a casual spot serving authentic Greek cuisine. The restaurant is known for its friendly service and excellent local dishes. With views of the marina, it's a great place to enjoy a relaxed meal.

Price Range: €15-€30 per person

Must-Try: Stuffed vine leaves, grilled meats, and feta cheese drizzled with honey.

Seaside Dining Experiences

Dining by the sea is one of the highlights of visiting Kos. Here are some of the best beachside restaurants offering incredible views and delicious food:

Akti Beach Bar and Restaurant

Located on Tigaki Beach, Akti Beach Bar offers a laid-back dining experience with stunning views of the sunset over the Aegean. The menu features fresh seafood, Mediterranean salads, and creative cocktails, making it a popular spot for both lunch and dinner.

Ambiance: Relaxed, with beachside seating and a casual vibe.

Menu Highlights: Grilled seafood platter, Greek salad, and seafood pasta.

Limnionas Fish Tavern

This secluded spot near Limnionas Beach is perfect for those looking to escape the crowds and enjoy fresh, locally caught seafood. The taverna offers simple yet delicious dishes, served with a backdrop of the rugged coastline.

Ambiance: Quiet and rustic, with a peaceful, off-the-beaten-path vibe.

Menu Highlights: Grilled fish of the day, fried calamari, and traditional Greek meze.

Agios Stefanos Beach Bar

Located on Agios Stefanos Beach, this casual beach bar is ideal for those looking to enjoy a meal or drink with their toes in the sand. With its relaxed atmosphere and fresh menu, it's perfect for a laid-back lunch or sunset cocktails.

Ambiance: Beachfront, casual, and perfect for unwinding after a swim.

Menu Highlights: Fresh seafood, mezze platters, and refreshing drinks.

Wineries and Wine Bars

Kos's growing wine scene is an exciting part of its culinary landscape. These wineries and wine bars are the best places to explore the local wine culture:

Triantafyllopoulos Winery (KTIMA AKRANI)

Located near Kos Town, Triantafyllopoulos Winery is one of the island's leading producers of wine. The winery offers tours and tastings, allowing visitors to sample a range of wines made from local grape varieties. The vineyard's beautiful setting makes it an ideal place to spend an afternoon.

Must-Try: Assyrtiko and Malagousia white wines.

Petra Marinou Winery

Situated in Mastichari, Petra Marinou Winery is a small, family-run operation focusing on organic wine production. The winery offers guided tours and tastings, where visitors can learn about local winemaking traditions and enjoy the fruits of the land.

Must-Try: Full-bodied red wines made from indigenous grape varieties.

Plori Wine Bar

Located in Kos Town, Plori Wine Bar offers a curated selection of local and international wines. With a cozy, laid-back atmosphere, it's the perfect spot for an evening of wine tasting accompanied by small plates of local cheeses and cured meats.

Must-Try: Kos wines paired with meze.

Local Markets and Specialty Foods

Kos has vibrant markets where you can find fresh produce, local products, and traditional foods. Here's where to shop for authentic local ingredients:

Kos Town Market

Located in Eleftherias Square, Kos Town Market is the go-to spot for fresh produce, herbs, spices, and local delicacies. The market offers a wide range of goods, including fruits, vegetables, artisanal cheeses, olive oil, and honey. It's the perfect place to pick up ingredients for a picnic or authentic souvenirs to bring home.

Must-Try: Local honey, olive oil, and fresh herbs.

Mastichari Local Market

Situated in the village of Mastichari, this market is known for its fresh seafood and locally produced goods. Vendors sell everything from freshly caught fish to homemade bread, pastries, and traditional sweets. It's a great place to explore the flavors of Kos.

Must-Try: Fresh seafood, artisanal breads, and local sweets.

Specialty Foods

Chapter 7: Nightlife

Kos Town bars and clubs

1. Jackson's Beach Bar

Jackson's Beach Bar is a lively, beachfront venue offering a fun mix of music, cocktails, and a laid-back atmosphere. Located right by the water, it's a great place to start your evening, enjoying drinks with stunning views of the sea. The bar is known for its vibrant sunset vibe and offers both indoor and outdoor seating. DJs often play upbeat music as the night progresses, turning it into a buzzing party spot.

Ambiance: Relaxed during the day, lively at night with a mix of beach bar and club atmosphere.

Must-Try Drink: Their signature mojitos and refreshing frozen cocktails.

2. Zero Cafe Bar

Located in the heart of Kos Town, Zero Cafe Bar is one of the most popular spots for both locals and tourists. The bar offers a stylish, modern ambiance with comfortable outdoor seating, perfect for people-watching. It's known for its excellent selection of cocktails, including both classic and creative concoctions. As the night continues, the bar fills up with a lively crowd, and the music becomes more energetic, making it a great spot for pre-club drinks.

Ambiance: Trendy, relaxed, and perfect for an early evening drink.

Must-Try Drink: Their wide range of gin-based cocktails.

3. Mylos Beach Bar & Club

Mylos Beach Bar & Club is a unique venue located on Lambi Beach, just a short walk from Kos Town. Set around an old windmill, this beach bar transforms into a nightclub as the sun goes down. It's known for hosting some of the best summer parties on the island, featuring live DJs, themed nights, and beachside dancing. During the day, it's a relaxing spot for drinks, but at night it turns into one of the hottest spots for clubbing.

Ambiance: Chill during the day, full-on beach party vibe at night.

Must-Try Drink: Tropical cocktails and signature summer punches.

4. Hamam Club

Hamam Club is a well-known nightclub in Kos Town, offering a vibrant nightlife experience with a unique atmosphere. The club is located inside a beautifully restored Turkish bathhouse, which adds to the exotic feel of the venue. Hamam Club is famous for its upbeat house and electronic music, with top DJs performing regularly. The club has multiple rooms, each with a different music vibe, making it a versatile spot for those who want to dance the night away.

Ambiance: Eclectic and stylish, with a lively and energetic crowd.

Must-Try Drink: Classic cocktails and premium spirits.

5. Artemis Heaven Beach-Bar

One of the largest and most popular nightclubs in Kos, Heaven Club is where you'll find the biggest parties. Located on the edge of Kos Town's bar street, this club is known for its booming sound system, international DJs, and dance floor that fills up quickly as the night goes on. The venue hosts themed events, foam parties, and guest DJ performances throughout the summer, making it a must-visit for those who love to party.

Ambiance: High-energy with a vibrant, youthful crowd.

Must-Try Drink: Classic mixers and energy drinks to keep the party going.

6. Camel Bar

Situated along the harbor in Kos Town, Camel Bar is a well-established spot that offers both daytime relaxation and nighttime fun. By day, it's a chilled bar where you can enjoy a cold drink while watching the boats in the marina. At night, it turns into a lively venue with upbeat music and a dance floor. The bar has a loyal following and is popular with both locals and tourists. Its central location makes it a great place to start your night.

Ambiance: Casual during the day, energetic with great music at night.

Must-Try Drink: Try one of their classic cocktails or a cold beer to kick off the night.

7. **Sitar Cocktail Bar**

Sitar Cocktail Bar offers a more relaxed, sophisticated nightlife option in Kos Town. Known for its laid-back atmosphere and stylish decor, it's the perfect spot for those who prefer to enjoy expertly crafted cocktails in a chill setting. The bar has an extensive cocktail menu with both classic and innovative drinks, all made with premium spirits and fresh ingredients. It's a quieter option for starting or ending your night in Kos Town.

Ambiance: Relaxed and elegant, perfect for cocktail enthusiasts.

Must-Try Drink: Signature cocktails like the Sitar Special and the Aegean Breeze.

8. West Bar

A popular bar on Kos Town's famous bar street, West Bar is known for its lively atmosphere, energetic music, and fantastic drink specials. The bar has a loyal crowd, especially among younger visitors, and is a great place to enjoy a more casual night out. As the night progresses, the music gets louder, and the bar turns into a mini-club with people dancing inside and outside.

Ambiance: Lively, energetic, and perfect for budget-conscious partygoers.

Must-Try Drink: Shots and mixed drinks are the go-to here.

Kardamena nightlife

Kardamena, located on the southern coast of Kos, is known for its energetic and diverse nightlife scene. With bars, clubs, beach parties, and cocktail lounges, it's a hotspot for visitors looking to enjoy a night out by the sea. Whether you're in the mood for dancing, live music, or sipping cocktails under the stars, Kardamena has something for everyone.

Beach Parties and Events

Kardamena is famous for its beach parties and summer events, where the fun spills out onto the sand. Here are some of the best parties and events to experience:

Full Moon Parties

Kardamena hosts lively Full Moon Parties, particularly during the summer season. These events, held at beachfront bars like Mylos and others, feature live DJ sets, bonfires, and a wild party atmosphere that lasts until dawn. The Full Moon Parties are legendary for their vibrant energy, bringing together travelers from all over the world to dance under the moonlight.

Beach Festivals

During the summer, Kardamena plays host to several beach festivals, featuring live music, international DJs, and beach games. These festivals attract a diverse crowd and are known for their electric atmosphere. Popular venues for these festivals include Mylos Beach Bar and other seaside venues, where the sandy shores serve as the perfect dance floor.

Live Music Performances

Many of the bars and beach clubs in Kardamena feature live music performances throughout the week. You'll find everything from acoustic sets to full-band performances covering rock, pop, and Greek music. The Beach House is one such venue known for hosting live acts and creating a chill, laid-back vibe perfect for enjoying drinks by the sea.

Tips and Insights

Best Nights to Go Out: The nightlife in Kardamena is in full swing during the summer months, with Fridays and Saturdays being the busiest. For a more relaxed vibe, midweek nights can be just as fun, especially for beach bars and lounges.

Dress Code and Entry Policies: Most bars and clubs in Kardamena have a casual dress code, with beach attire acceptable at many venues. However, for nightclubs like Q Club, it's best to dress smart-casual. Entry fees vary, with most clubs charging between €5-€10, often including a free drink.

Safety and Responsible Drinking: Kardamena is generally safe, but it's important to stay aware of your surroundings, especially in crowded clubs and bars. Drink responsibly, and always keep an eye on your belongings. Taxis are easily available for safe transportation back to your hotel.

Local Insights: Kardamena's nightlife often extends until dawn, so pace yourself! Bar Street is a great place to start the night, and many venues offer drink specials early in the evening. Beach parties are also an unforgettable way to experience the island's vibrant social scene, so be sure to ask around for upcoming events during your stay.

Beach Bars at Paradise Beach and Tigaki

1. Paradise Beach Bars

Paradise Beach, located on the southern coast of Kos, is not only famous for its crystal-clear waters and soft sand but also for its vibrant beach bars. During the day, these spots are perfect for sunbathing with a refreshing drink in hand, while at night they transform into lively social hubs. Some of the best beach bars include:

Banana Beach Bar: Situated right on Paradise Beach, this beach bar offers a laid-back atmosphere during the day with sunbeds and parasols available for rent. As the sun sets, it becomes a lively spot with great music, signature cocktails, and beachside vibes.

Paradise Beach Bar: Known for its tropical cocktails and beach parties, this bar is perfect for those looking to enjoy a fun night out after a day of sun and sea. The drinks menu includes everything from fresh smoothies to rum-based cocktails.

2. Tigaki Beach Bars

Tigaki Beach offers a more relaxed vibe compared to Paradise Beach, but its beach bars still provide a great mix of chill and fun:

Esperos Beach Bar: Located right on Tigaki Beach, Esperos offers sunbeds by day and cocktails by night. The bar is popular for its relaxed ambiance and breathtaking sunset views. Try their signature cocktails while you watch the waves roll in.

Ipanema Beach Bar: Ipanema is known for its beachfront seating and wide range of drinks, including classic cocktails and refreshing iced coffees. As the sun goes down, the vibe picks up with music and friendly crowds.

Cocktail Spots in Zia

Zia Village is best known for its stunning sunset views and traditional Greek atmosphere, but it's also home to some excellent cocktail spots that make for a perfect evening in the mountains:

Oromedon Taverna

One of the most iconic places in Zia, Oromedon Taverna offers not only incredible views over Kos but also a fantastic cocktail menu. The rooftop terrace is the ideal spot to sip a cocktail while watching the sun set behind the Aegean Sea. Their signature drinks are made with local spirits and fresh ingredients.

Sunset Balcony Tavern

As the name suggests, Sunset Balcony Bar is all about the views. Located at one of the highest points in Zia, this spot offers breathtaking sunset views and a great cocktail list. The atmosphere is relaxed, with a focus on enjoying the moment with a refreshing drink in hand. Try their "Zia Sunset" cocktail, made with fresh citrus and local honey.

Relaxed Nightlife Options

For those seeking a more low-key evening, Kos has several options that offer a relaxing nightlife experience without the club scene:

Yacht Café Kos (Kos Town)

Located by the marina in Kos Town, Yacht Café offers a chill vibe with comfortable seating and beautiful views of the boats in the harbor. It's perfect for an evening of quiet conversation over drinks or coffee. The bar serves a wide range of cocktails, coffees, and snacks, making it an ideal spot for a laid-back night.

Sitar Cocktail Bar (Kos Town)

Known for its creative cocktails and sophisticated setting, Sitar Cocktail Bar is the place to go for a more relaxed yet stylish evening. With cozy outdoor seating, ambient lighting, and a carefully crafted drinks menu, this bar is perfect for those who want to enjoy a quiet, atmospheric night out.

Zero Cafe

For a more casual evening, Zero Cafe offers a great mix of coffee, cocktails, and light bites. The setting is calm and inviting, making it a great option for those looking to unwind with a drink or two while enjoying the island's easy-going atmosphere.

Chapter 8: Shopping

Souvenir Shopping in Kos Town

Kos Town is the perfect place to start your shopping journey. Its narrow streets are lined with shops and stalls offering a wide range of souvenirs, traditional products, and unique mementos that will remind you of your time on the island.

Top Souvenir Shops

Agora Souvenir Shop: Located near Eleftherias Square, Agora is a well-known shop offering a wide selection of traditional Greek products. From ceramics and handmade jewelry to olive oil and local wines, this shop is perfect for finding quality souvenirs.

Kosmos Handmade Crafts: Specializing in local handicrafts, Kosmos is the place to find unique, handmade items such as woven baskets, embroidered linens, and hand-painted ceramics. These make beautiful gifts or keepsakes.

The Olive Tree Shop: This shop focuses on products made from olive wood, including kitchen utensils, cutting boards, and decorative items. Each piece is unique and offers a piece of Greece's natural beauty to take home.

Tips for Authentic Souvenirs: Look for items like locally produced olive oil, handmade ceramics, leather sandals, and traditional Greek worry beads (komboloi). For authentic products, avoid generic souvenir stands and explore shops that emphasize local craftsmanship.

Local Markets for Traditional Products

Kos's local markets are a must-visit for those looking to experience the island's culture and buy fresh, authentic products. Here are the best markets to explore:

Kos Town Market

Located in Eleftherias Square, Kos Town Market is a bustling hub for fresh produce, herbs, spices, and local delicacies. Stalls overflow with seasonal fruits, vegetables, and a variety of herbs like oregano and thyme. You can also find local cheeses, olive oil, and honey, all produced on the island.

Kardamena Market

Kardamena's local market is smaller but offers a great selection of traditional products. It's a great place to find fresh fish, local wine, and artisanal bread. If you're looking to buy local delicacies, this market offers an authentic shopping experience away from the busier tourist spots.

Tigaki Market

The Tigaki Market is known for its variety of fresh produce and local food products. You'll find island-grown fruits, homemade jams, and fresh herbs. It's a great spot for picking up high-quality olive oil and locally made snacks like loukoumades (Greek honey doughnuts) and cheese pies.

Local Specialties: When shopping at the markets, be sure to pick up fresh produce, local herbs, and handmade textiles like tablecloths and scarves. These products are perfect for bringing a taste of Kos back home.

Zia Village

Zia Village is not only known for its stunning sunset views but also for its traditional shops and local artisans. It's a charming village with cobbled streets filled with small stores offering authentic Greek products and handmade crafts.

Traditional Shops: Zia is home to many family-run shops where you can find items like pottery, woven rugs, honey, and herbal soaps. These shops provide a more intimate shopping experience, often with the artisans themselves explaining their craft.

Local Artisans: Many of the products sold in Zia are handmade by local artisans. From hand-painted ceramics to embroidered linens, every piece tells a story of Greek craftsmanship. The village is particularly famous for its pottery, and you'll find many shops selling beautiful vases and dishes in traditional Greek designs.

Scenic Views: Shopping in Zia is a unique experience due to the breathtaking views. Many shops are perched on the hillside, offering panoramic views of the surrounding landscape while you shop. It's the perfect place to enjoy a drink at a café after browsing the local stores.

Boutique Shops in Kardamena and Tigaki

For fashion and accessories, Kardamena and Tigaki have a number of boutique shops where you can find stylish clothing, jewelry, and home decor.

Kardamena Boutiques: Kardamena is home to several small, stylish boutiques that offer Greek fashion and accessories. Shops like The White Pearl feature locally designed clothing, perfect for picking up a chic summer outfit. You'll also find stores selling handmade jewelry and unique accessories that reflect the island's laid-back style.

Tigaki Boutiques: In Tigaki, you'll find small shops offering resort wear, bathing suits, and fashionable summer accessories. The boutiques here are ideal for beachgoers looking for high-quality beachwear and gifts. You can also discover unique home decor items, such as handcrafted cushions and rugs, perfect for adding a touch of Greek island charm to your home.

Olive Oil, Wine, and Local Delicacies

No shopping experience in Kos is complete without indulging in the island's culinary delights. Kos is known for its high-quality olive oil, locally produced wines, and traditional delicacies like honey and spices.

Where to Buy Olive Oil: Kos Town Market and Zia Village are great places to find premium olive oil. Look for extra virgin olive oil from local farms, often sold in small family-run shops. Many shops offer tastings, so you can sample different varieties before making your purchase.

Local Wines: Triantafyllopoulos Winery (KTIMA AKRANI) and Petra Marinou Winery in Mastichari are the best places to buy Kos's finest wines. Both wineries offer tours and tastings, allowing visitors to experience the unique flavors of Kos wine. Be sure to try the island's Assyrtiko and Malagousia wines, both excellent examples of Greek white wines.

Traditional Delicacies: Local honey, herbs, and spices are sold in most markets and specialty food stores across the island. Look for thyme honey, a local favorite, as well as herbs like oregano and mountain tea. These items make perfect gifts or culinary souvenirs to bring home.

Tasting and Selection Tips: When selecting olive oil, look for cold-pressed, extra virgin varieties for the best flavor and quality. For wine, many shops and wineries offer tastings, so take the opportunity to sample a few different types before choosing your favorite. When buying local delicacies, shop early for the freshest produce, and don't hesitate to ask vendors for advice on the best products.

Chapter 9: Itineraries

3-Day Itinerary

Day 1: Kos Town and Hidden Gems

Morning: Begin your trip with a leisurely stroll through Kos Town, starting at Nerantzia Castle (Castle of the Knights). Explore the medieval fortress, then head to the Roman Odeon, a well-preserved amphitheater with fascinating ancient architecture.

Lunch: Enjoy lunch at Alberto's Restaurant, a popular spot near the waterfront that serves Greek classics and fresh seafood.

Afternoon: Spend time at Hippocrates Tree and the Archaeological Museum of Kos to dive into the island's rich history. Walk through the charming Ancient Agora, filled with ruins and remnants of Kos's past.

Evening: Enjoy a sunset cocktail at Yacht Café Kos, located by the marina, and have dinner at Platanos Restaurant for a mix of Greek and Mediterranean cuisine.

Day 2: Paradise Beach and Boat Adventure

Morning: Spend a relaxing morning at Paradise Beach. You can sunbathe, swim, or enjoy water sports like paddleboarding and jet skiing.

Lunch: Enjoy a laid-back lunch at Banana Beach Bar with views of the sea and refreshing cocktails.

Afternoon: Take a boat tour from Paradise Beach to explore nearby coves and islands, with stops for swimming and snorkeling. Many boat trips include stops at hidden beaches and sea caves.

Evening: Return to Kos Town for a seafood dinner at Barbouni, followed by a cocktail at Camel Bar, where you can enjoy harbor views.

Day 3: Zia Village and Mountain Views

Morning: Drive up to Zia Village, a charming mountainside spot known for its local handicrafts, traditional shops, and scenic views. Wander through the village and explore the artisanal stores, where you can buy handmade pottery, herbs, and textiles.

Lunch: Enjoy lunch at Oromedon Taverna, a family-run restaurant with stunning panoramic views over the island.

Afternoon: Hike the nearby trails of Mount Dikeos for stunning views, or take a scenic walk around the village.

Evening: Stay in Zia to experience the famous sunset from Sunset Balcony Bar, followed by dinner at Taverna Fantasia, known for its local dishes and warm atmosphere.

5-Day Itinerary

Day 1: Kefalos and Beach Day

Morning: Head to Kefalos, a picturesque village perched on a hill with views of the coast. Visit the Basilica of Agios Stefanos and stroll through the quaint village streets.

Lunch: Enjoy a seafood lunch at Kastri Taverna, located near Agios Stefanos Beach, where you can take in views of Kastri Islet.

Afternoon: Spend the rest of the afternoon at Camel Beach or Limnionas Beach, known for their tranquil atmospheres. Relax, swim, or try snorkeling.

Evening: Return to Kardamena for a casual dinner at a beachside taverna, such as Avli.

Day 2: Village Hopping and Culture

Morning: Start your day with a visit to Antimachia, a traditional village known for its windmill and nearby Antimachia Castle. Explore the windmill and learn about local traditions.

Lunch: Stop for a light lunch at a taverna in Antimachia, such as Traditional House of Antimachia.

Afternoon: Visit Paleo Pili, an abandoned medieval village nestled in the mountains. Hike up to the ruins of the old castle and take in the panoramic views of the island.

Evening: Have dinner in Tigaki, where you can enjoy a beachside meal at Esperos Beach Bar and stay to watch the sunset.

Day 3: Thermal Springs and Tigaki Beach

Morning: Visit Therma Beach (Embros Therme), known for its natural hot springs. Spend the morning relaxing in the warm waters surrounded by dramatic cliffs.

Lunch: Head to a nearby taverna, such as Agios Fokas Tavern, for a traditional Greek lunch.

Afternoon: Spend the rest of the afternoon at Tigaki Beach, known for its long stretch of soft sand and calm waters. It's a great place to swim, sunbathe, or try windsurfing.

Evening: Enjoy dinner at Meni, a beachfront restaurant in Tigaki with a casual, welcoming vibe.

Day 4: Wineries and Kos Town Evening

Morning: Visit Triantafyllopoulos Winery (KTIMA AKRANI) for a wine tasting tour. Explore the vineyard, learn about the winemaking process, and sample local wines.

Lunch: Enjoy a light lunch at the winery or stop at a local taverna in Mastichari.

Afternoon: Spend your afternoon back in Kos Town, visiting hidden gems like the Western Archaeological Zone.

Evening: Enjoy an elegant dinner at Elia, followed by drinks at Plori Wine Bar for a relaxed evening.

Day 5: Day Trip to Nisyros Island

Morning: Take a boat trip from Kos Town to Nisyros, a volcanic island nearby. Once there, visit the volcanic crater and explore Nikia Village, known for its beautiful architecture and views.

Lunch: Have lunch at a local taverna in Mandraki, the main village, overlooking the sea.

Afternoon: Continue exploring Nisyros, visiting the Volcanological Museum or relaxing by the sea before returning to Kos in the evening.

Evening: Enjoy a farewell dinner at Oromedon Taverna in Zia Village for a sunset experience before heading home.

7-Day Itinerary

Day 1: Kos Town and Western Archaeological Zone

Morning: Begin your trip in Kos Town, visiting the Western Archaeological Zone, which includes ancient Roman houses, the remains of temples, and mosaics.

Lunch: Have lunch at Zero Café Bar in Kos Town for a casual bite.

Afternoon: Spend the afternoon visiting Nerantzia Castle and walking through the Ancient Agora.

Evening: Enjoy a dinner at Platanos, known for its central location and classic Greek menu.

Day 2: Lambi Beach and Local Markets

Morning: Relax at Lambi Beach, close to Kos Town, with soft sand and calm waters. It's a great place for sunbathing and swimming.

Lunch: Grab a beachfront lunch at Mylos Beach Bar.

Afternoon: Visit the Kos Town Market for local products like honey, herbs, and olive oil.

Evening: Enjoy dinner at Barbouni, with fresh seafood and harbor views.

Day 3: Full-Day Boat Trip

Morning: Spend the day on a full-day boat trip around Kos and nearby islands. Stop at Kalymnos Island to explore its sponge-diving culture and enjoy a swim in hidden coves.

Lunch: Enjoy lunch on board the boat or at a taverna in Pserimos.

Afternoon: Continue the boat trip, with stops for snorkeling and beach visits.

Evening: Return to Kos Town for a casual dinner at Taverna Petrino.

Day 4: Explore Kardamena and Mylotopi

Morning: Visit Kardamena, a lively seaside town with a mix of bars, shops, and restaurants. Explore the local boutiques and enjoy a morning coffee.

Lunch: Have lunch at Skala Café & Cocktails on the beachfront.

Afternoon: Visit Mylotopi, where you can see a traditional windmill and a folklore museum. Learn about local history and enjoy the scenic views.

Evening: Have dinner at Pelagos, located in Kardamena, known for its delicious seafood dishes.

Day 5: Hiking in Mount Dikeos

Morning: Start your day with a hike to the peak of Mount Dikeos, where you'll be rewarded with breathtaking views of the entire island.

Lunch: Enjoy lunch at a taverna in Asfendiou Village, such as Taverna Asfendiou.

Afternoon: Relax in Zia Village after your hike, exploring its charming shops and cafés.

Evening: Stay in Zia for dinner at Taverna Fantasia and enjoy the sunset.

Day 6: Wineries and Beach Time

Morning: Visit Petra Marinou Winery in Mastichari for a tour and wine tasting.

Lunch: Enjoy lunch at a nearby taverna in Mastichari.

Afternoon: Spend the rest of the afternoon at Mastichari Beach, known for its soft sand and excellent windsurfing conditions.

Evening: Return to Kos Town for a relaxing dinner at Oromedon Taverna in Zia.

Day 7: Plaka Forest and Departure

Morning: Visit Plaka Forest to see the peacocks and enjoy a peaceful walk through the shaded forest.

Lunch: Have a final lunch at a taverna near Tigaki Beach, such as Esperos Beach Bar.

Afternoon: Spend your last hours relaxing at Tigaki Beach before heading back to the airport for your departure.

Conclusion

As we wrap up this journey through the enchanting island of Kos, it's clear that this Greek gem offers something special for every type of traveler. Whether you've wandered through ancient ruins, relaxed on pristine beaches, explored charming mountain villages, or experienced the vibrant nightlife, Kos is an island that leaves a lasting impression.

From the rich history found in Kos Town and Asklepion to the scenic beauty of Zia Village and the sun-soaked sands of Paradise Beach, Kos is a blend of the old and new, the relaxing and the adventurous. The local food and wine provide a true taste of the island's culture, while the warm hospitality of its people invites you to linger a little longer.

No matter how you choose to spend your days—hiking the trails of Mount Dikeos, exploring hidden beaches, or simply savoring the fresh flavors of Greek cuisine—Kos offers endless opportunities to create unforgettable memories. As you leave, you'll take a piece of Kos with you, whether in the form of a special souvenir, a new favorite dish, or a beautiful sunset forever imprinted in your mind.

Thank you for allowing us to guide you through this journey. May your time in Kos be as enriching and fulfilling as this remarkable island deserves. Safe travels, and until we meet again, Καλό ταξίδι!

Printed in Great Britain
by Amazon

55564322R00076